The CRIMSON Thread

a play in three acts

by

Mary Hanes

SAMUEL FRENCH, INC.

45 WEST 25TH STREET   NEW YORK 10010
7623 SUNSET BOULEVARD   HOLLYWOOD 90046
LONDON   TORONTO

IMPORTANT BILLING AND CREDIT REQUIREMENTS

Kathleen Noone and Stephanie Zimbalist
in Act I of THE CRIMSON THREAD at
Seven Angels Theatre.

THE CRIMSON THREAD was first presented on stage at Seven Angels Theater; Semina De Laurentis, Artistic Director; at the Hamiton Pavilion Performing Arts Center in Waterbury, Connecticut, on May 5, 1994. The set was designed by Thomas Cariello, lighting by Gene Lenahan, costumes by Donna Trelford Fontana, and sound by Patrick Barrett and Jack Nardi. The production stage manager was Tammy Taylor. THE CRIMSON THREAD was directed by Dan Lauria with the following cast:

ACT I

Eilís McDermott Connelly ....Stephanie Zimbalist
Bridget McDermott Flynn ....Kathleen Noone

ACT II

Kathleen Connelly Wright ....Shanna Reed
Fionnuala Connelly Kennedy ....Stephanie Zimbalist

ACT III

Maggie Kennedy ....Kathleen Noone
Nora Kennedy Fitzpatrick ....Shanna Reed

Producers Gatien Lauria Productions, Kathleen Noone, Shanna Reed and Stephanie Zimbalist moved THE CRIMSON THREAD intact to the Pasadena Playhouse; Lars Hansen, Executive Director; Pasadena, California, where it opened on September 18, 1994.

For Ken

ACT I
Dun Laoghaire, Ireland
1869

(Setting: August, 1869, in the county outside of Dun Laoghaire, Ireland. The front of a cottage built of sod with a thatched roof is upstage right. Upstage left is a clothesline with several pieces of children's clothing hung from it. There are two worn wooden chairs on either side of a wood table in front of the cottage. On the table is a basket full of spools of thread, pieces of material and a dress. There is a Dutch door with a narrow sill on the bottom part of the door. The top of the door is open as is the window to the right of the door. The floor outside the cottage is dirt. EILÍS McDERMOTT CONNELLY sits on one of the wooden chairs sewing, although her thoughts are a million miles away. She wears a tattered dress and apron and is barefoot. She looks offstage and jumps up as BRIDGET McDERMOTT FLYNN enters. Bridget is Eilís' older sister and is 8-1/2 months pregnant. She is dressed similarly to Eilís and carries two large baskets of vegetables.)

EILÍS. Bridget! *(BRIDGET struggles with her baskets.*

EILÍS meets up with her and takes them.) Look at you—all weighed down. Let me help you with those baskets.

(EILÍS sets the baskets down.)

BRIDGET. Ta, Eilís.

(EILÍS pulls up a chair for BRIDGET.)

EILÍS. You sit here and rest yourself.
BRIDGET. *(Sits.)* My feet are most very grateful to you. *(Reaches into her pocket and pulls out a letter.)* Oh, I've your post here. It's a letter from your Daniel.

(EILÍS stops dead in her tracks. She reluctantly takes the letter from BRIDGET and stares at it.)

EILÍS. When'd it come?
BRIDGET. Just this mornin'. I ran into Jacob down at market. He was goin' to take it to you tomorrow, but I told him I'd take it to you directly—save him the trip.
EILÍS. I'm sure that made him happy. That old bicycle of his makes climbin' our hill like climbin' a mountain. Don't know why he even uses the contraption.
BRIDGET. For company I expect. He always winds up walkin' it beside him like a dear friend. *(They laugh at the thought of it. Pause.)* Well, aren't you goin' to open your letter, Eilís?

(EILÍS quickly stuffs the letter into her apron pocket.)

EILÍS. I'll read it later. Right now I just want to have a visit with you.

BRIDGET. What's goin' on?

EILÍS. Nothin'.

BRIDGET. Used to be a time when you'd rip it open and pour over every word till you'd committed it to memory. You've repeated many a letter to me word for word without once glancin' at the paper it was written on.

EILÍS. I haven't done that for a long time.

BRIDGET. That's true. *(Pause.)* I must say, I've been wonderin' why that is.

EILÍS. Not that much to tell really.

BRIDGET. I doubt that.

EILÍS. *(Exiting into house.)* I'll put up some tea.

BRIDGET. *(Yells.)* Daniel's letters have always been full of adventure. *(To herself.)* Ah, America. Every day a brand new world revealin' just a little bit more of its treasures. *(Pause. Yells.)* Please, Eilís, I reckon I could use some cheerin'. Read it to me, won't you?

EILÍS. *(O.S., Changes the subject.)* The only reason you need cheerin' is because you've exhausted yourself again. You're always doin' too much. You shouldn't have weighted yourself down with all those provisions!

BRIDGET. I hadn't planned on makin' this many purchases, but the prices were a little better, so I thought I'd best take advantage of it.

(EILÍS enters.)

EILÍS. Still, all by your lonesome—

BRIDGET. Truth be known. I just couldn't pass up the chance to have a wee bit of time to myself.

EILÍS. But you know you shouldn't be liftin' such heavy things this late in your time.

BRIDGET. It didn't stop me with the other five, and they turned out all right.

EILÍS. You didn't have the others as close as this one's comin'. You need someone helpin' you. Especially with Robert bein' sick. *(Pause.)* And how are you feelin'?

BRIDGET. Baby's been kickin' me all the way from the Davis' farm. Don't think it'll be too much longer before he's upon us. He seems to have quieted down now. I guess he must 'ave worn himself out.

EILÍS. Still so sure it's goin' to be a boy?

BRIDGET. Hopin's more likely. We're in desperate need of another hand in the field.

(EILÍS looks in baskets.)

EILÍS. All these for you?

BRIDGET. Mostly, but I had to pick up a few things for Ma.

EILÍS. If you'd just said the word, I could've helped you.

BRIDGET. Stop fussin' over me.

EILÍS. Until your little farm hand arrives, you let me do your fetchin' for you.

BRIDGET. You've plenty enough to fill your days.

EILÍS. I'm insistin', and nothin' will turn me from it.

BRIDGET. All right, Eilís.

EILÍS. Better yet, you give me a list before you leave, and

Kathleen and I will go for you on Tuesday next.

BRIDGET. All right.

EILÍS. You promise?

BRIDGET. Yes, I promise. Now stop your naggin' at me.

EILÍS. I'll help you home with your baskets after you've had a chance to rest a while. Come sit with me a bit while I do my sewin'.

BRIDGET. *(Removes a few wilted sugar beets from her basket.)* I tell ya, Mother is goin' to faint at the sight of these sugar beets. I'll have to disguise their appearance in my stew. God must've invented gravy for the poor. That way we can't really taste the food we're eatin'.

EILÍS. I think you're right.

BRIDGET. What've you got there?

EILÍS. I'm mendin' this dress for Kathleen again. I must've resewn it at least six times. *(Holds it up and studies the dress with its many different pieces of material.)* I'm not even sure which was the original material. Kathleen never complains though.

BRIDGET. She's got the sweetest temperament that girl.

EILÍS. Bein' the first, I thought they'd all be that calm. But I soon found that Kathleen was the exception.

BRIDGET. Count yourself lucky. I've had no exceptions!

EILÍS. She's been such a source of strength to me since Daniel left.

BRIDGET. She reminds me so much of her father.

EILÍS. Do you think?

BRIDGET. Aye, her spirit's the same as Daniel's—such quiet resolve—no matter what's goin' on around her.

EILÍS. I've come to depend on her so. And the way she looks after her brothers and Fionnuala. She's so good with all the children.

BRIDGET. Such a blessin' your Kathleen.

EILÍS. I hope I haven't burdened her too much. She's always in the kitchen with me churnin' butter, or out searchin' for snails or gatherin' wild whortleberries.

BRIDGET. I don't believe Kathleen would have it any other way.

EILÍS. I'm not so sure. There are moments when I catch a glimpse of the little girl in her. It's a thing she hides from me, I think.

BRIDGET. How do you mean?

EILÍS. I've seen her watchin' Fionnuala playin' with her rag doll, and I sense a great sadness in her. I wish I could give her back her childhood.

BRIDGET. None of us ever gets that back, thank God. *(Pause.)* Remember when we were little—durin' the worst years of the famine? Cryin' ourselves to sleep for lack of food in our bellies. You and I, wrappin' around each other in the night so as not to freeze. Bein' a child back then was like a terrible dream that you couldn't wake yourself from.

EILÍS. Daniel vowed our children would have a better life. *(With a faraway look.)* It's what made him leave.

BRIDGET. I wish you'd read that letter. I'd hate to think I saved Jacob the trip for naught.

EILÍS. I left it inside.

BRIDGET. Shall I get it?

EILÍS. No. You stay put. *(Again changes the subject.)* Oh, I almost forgot. Rebecca O'Reilly came visitin' today. Father

O'Neal has asked her to take up another collection.

BRIDGET. I am so tired of the church askin' for money when they know full well there's none to give. Where's the church when the landlord comes demandin' his share I'd like to know!

EILÍS. Bridget, I won't listen to that talk of yours.

BRIDGET. Listen or not, it's the way it is.

EILÍS. Enough! Now do you want that cup of tea?

BRIDGET. That would be lovely.

EILÍS. I'll get it then.

(EILÍS exits into the house. BRIDGET gently strokes her stomach. She softly sings to the baby. As her song gets louder, it becomes obvious that this is no lullaby. It is an Irish rebel song, "God Save Ireland.")

BRIDGET. *(Sings.)* [1]

High upon the gallows tree swung the noble-hearted three,

By the vengeful tyrant stricken in their bloom;

But they met him face to face,

with the courage of their race,

And they went with souls undaunted to their doom.

(Chorus.)

"God save Ireland!" said the heroes;

"God save Ireland!" said they all.

"Whether on the scaffold high

---

[1] "God Save Ireland" Text: by T.D. Sullivan, published in Ireland's *The Nation*, December 7th, 1867. Tune: George Root's American march, "Tramp, tramp, tramp, the boys are marching." The song was often reprinted under the title, "The Manchester Patriot Martyrs."

BRIDGET. (Singing, cont.)
Or the battlefield we die,
O, what matter when for Ireland dear we fall!"

Never till the latest day shall the memory pass away
Of the gallant lives thus given for our land;
But on the cause must go, amid joy or weal or woe,
Till we make this Isle a Nation free and grand.
(Chorus.)
"God save Ireland!" said the heroes;
"God save Ireland!" said they all.
"Whether on the scaffold high
Or the...

(BRIDGET abruptly stops singing as EILÍS returns with the tea.)

EILÍS. What are you singin' to your wee one?
BRIDGET. Just a song I heard.
EILÍS. Where would you be learnin' a rebel song? And don't you think a lullaby would be more suitable?
BRIDGET. Not if I want to instill a little fight in him before he's born. Get the wheels turnin' so to speak.
EILÍS. Bridget, let him be born first before you start fillin' his head with such ideas.
BRIDGET. If you don't stir things up a bit, nothin' will change.
EILÍS. It's not so bad. We have our homes.
BRIDGET. This month maybe, but who knows about next. When the landlord owns your land you've got no say. In America you'll have rights—the right to own a piece of land

that no one will be able to take from you.

EILÍS. As long as I pay the rent, it's mine. That's enough.

BRIDGET. What about those who can't make the rent? What happens to them? They get tossed out. Swept away like nothin' more than cobwebs. The Duggan's got their notice yesterday. They'll have to be off the land tomorrow. Where are they supposed to go? Where would we go?

EILÍS. We've managed to make the rent thus far.

BRIDGET. But we're always in a struggle to do so. There may come a day when we're tossed off the land.

EILÍS. We'll face that when the time comes.

BRIDGET. And all the while, they keep raisin' the rent on us! Nothin' will really change until we've won the right to own our land.

EILÍS. You frighten me with all your rebellious talk.

BRIDGET. Ireland's changin', Eilís. Every day another step must be taken.

EILÍS. So I've been hearin'. Rebecca O'Reilly didn't come by just to talk about takin' up a collection.

BRIDGET. *(Avoids EILÍS' stare.)* Oh?

EILÍS. She filled my ear with a lot of stories about you and your recent activities. Where have you been goin' every Tuesday for the past month?

(BRIDGET goes to pour the tea.)

BRIDGET. I'll pour the tea.

EILÍS. Where'd you go this morning before market?

BRIDGET. I've been to a few of their meetins' is all. I greatly admire the Fenians, Eilís. They are courageous in the face of much sufferin'.

EILÍS. And they've asked nothin' of you?

BRIDGET. No.

EILÍS. But they will.

BRIDGET. They might.

EILÍS. Promise me you'll refuse to help them.

BRIDGET. I can't promise you that.

EILÍS. There's talk of the Pope excommunicatin' all its members.

BRIDGET. I must tell you, Eilís, I'm far more afraid of poverty than I am the Pope.

EILÍS. Shame on you! You're speakin' like you're already one of them! They are nothin' more than terrorists.

BRIDGET. They're fightin' for our rights—they're fightin' for us, Eilís! So that someday when we're pullin' up the sugar beets that we've planted—tended—cried over—we can say, "This is my land. I've the right to be here."

EILÍS. Ireland's covered in the blood from that struggle. Are you willin' to become one of their martyrs?

BRIDGET. I am careful.

EILÍS. So careful that Rebecca O'Reilly has come to me with tales of your involvement? She says you've given your soul to that lot of criminals. Is that true, Bridget?

BRIDGET. Is my soul too high a price to pay to guarantee that my children will have a future? They are not goin' to the land of promise like yours. Don't forget, Eilís, your tomorrows are gleamin' with opportunity. Here, I have to create my own. So don't pass judgment on me.

EILÍS. *(Pause.)* I'm not. It's just that you are as much a part of me as my arms or my legs or my heart.

BRIDGET. Then keep your faith in me. *(The baby suddenly kicks.)* Oh, Eilís, the baby's kickin' somethin' fierce.

You must feel this.

EILÍS. I've felt a baby before.

(BRIDGET grabs EILÍS' hand and places it on her stomach.)

BRIDGET. There he goes again. He's goin' to be a strong one, he is.

EILÍS. *(Softens.)* Another jewel for your necklace of children. Oh, Bridget, right now, right this very moment you look so beautiful. *(Pause.)* Fionnuala was just a heartbeat in my belly when Daniel left for America.

BRIDGET. He'll love her. She's quiet, but just behind her eyes you can see she's full of fire. It's just waitin' to reveal itself. And she's such a sense of wonder about everythin'. Always pleadin' with me to tell her another story. She loved hearin' about the fairies.

EILÍS. I suppose I should be happy you're tellin' her nicer stories.

BRIDGET. What do you mean?

EILÍS. She wouldn't go near the water for weeks after you told her about the "soul cages." About the mermaid who keeps the souls of shipwrecked victims in lobster pots at the bottom of the sea. Really, Bridget!

BRIDGET. I was merely tryin' to entertain her.

EILÍS. And now she's been talkin' about nothin' but fairies since she visited you.

BRIDGET. I can't help it if she loves my stories.

EILÍS. Every mornin' she runs out of the cottage to see if the fairies have drunk up all the dew from the blades of grass. Why do you fill her head with such silliness?

BRIDGET. Are they just silly stories, do you think?

EILÍS. Oh, Bridget!

BRIDGET. I believe I actually saw one the other day! He was standin' just outside my door—only a few inches high he was. I could see right through him. He was wearin' clothes spun of silver, and his wee cap was stitched with bright red flowers from the foxglove.

EILÍS. *(Sarcastically.)* May the saints preserve us!

BRIDGET. He asked about you!

EILÍS. *(Plays along.)* Oh, did he now?

BRIDGET. Yes. He asked me why you've been lookin' so weary of late. *(Thoughtfully.)* Why do you look so weary, Eilís?

EILÍS. Just tired is all. I didn't sleep much last night. Fionnuala got a bit of a cold yesterday and coughed most the night. She wouldn't let me leave her bedside. She's inside sleeping now.

BRIDGET. It's very quiet around here. Where's the rest of your brood?

EILÍS. Kathleen has rounded up the bunch of them, and they've gone off to the McLellan farm to await the birth of a new calf. If they're not back by dusk, I'll have to cross the field and fetch 'em. I hope that cow gives birth in a timely manner and saves me the trip.

(BRIDGET sips her tea.)

BRIDGET. I can't remember the last time it was this quiet.

EILÍS. How was Robert feelin' today?

BRIDGET. The same. His cough never leaves him a moment's peace. *(Pause.)* You're lucky Daniel went to work in America instead of the mines.

EILÍS. Robert just didn't want to go so far from his family.

He wanted to be able to come home from time to time to see you.

BRIDGET. And every time he came home, I got pregnant. Oh, Eilís, it's so hard seein' him so weak, and the doctor bills are adding up—

EILÍS. He'll get better, Bridget. *(Pause.)* I could scrape up a bit of money for the doctor.

(EILÍS exits into the house. BRIDGET calls after her.)

BRIDGET. Eilís, that's the money Daniel sent you for your trip to America. He's worked so hard for every bit of it. I can't take it from you.

(EILÍS reenters carrying a tin. She removes some coins and hands them to BRIDGET.)

EILÍS. I want you to take it.
BRIDGET. No, I can't.
EILÍS. I'm not handin' all of it to you, just a bit.
BRIDGET. He'll be angry with the both of us.
EILÍS. Then we won't tell him will we? He doesn't know exactly how much I have. I've been more frugal than he imagines. Please, Bridget, take it.

(BRIDGET finally takes the coins.)

BRIDGET. All right then, but I'll find a way to repay it.
EILÍS. It's no loan. I'm simply givin' some money to my favorite sister.
BRIDGET. I'm your only sister.

EILÍS. So you are. *(Pause.)* I want Robert to get better as much as you do.

BRIDGET. He did look a little better after he saw the Doctor this mornin'. *(Pause.)* When I left the house he actually patted me rump as I walked past him.

EILÍS. Now that's a good sign.

BRIDGET. Well, the mind is willin' but the body just can't seem to follow through, if you know what I mean.

EILÍS. After three years, I find it's not the act of it that I miss as much as just holdin' each other. It was as if our whole day was spent workin' toward that moment. Like it was our reward. We'd lie together and fall into each others dreams.

(BRIDGET laughs.)

BRIDGET. If Mother could hear us now. She'd faint from the shock.

EILÍS. Well, she faints easily. *(They laugh and toast their cups. Pause.)* Bridget, did you see last night's moon?

BRIDGET. Aye, it took up half the sky.

EILÍS. I was sittin' in the rocker by the window next to Fionnuala gazin' up at it half the night. It's glow lit up the room as if I'd the lamp goin'. It made me feel so small, and it started me thinkin' about the future—about what's out there for me—for us.

BRIDGET. *(With great difficulty.)* Why is Daniel writin' to you from Massachusetts?

EILÍS. How'd you know?

BRIDGET. The postmark. What's he doin' there?

EILÍS. Findin' us a house to live in.

BRIDGET. *(Pause.)* He's finally sendin' for you then.

EILÍS. Don't say it.

BRIDGET. But if it's true...

EILÍS. If you don't say it, it won't be true.

BRIDGET. I knew he'd send for you eventually. But the more time that passed, the less real it seemed.

EILÍS. He's a very determined man, and three years have not diminished that.

BRIDGET. I've seen somethin' stirrin' inside you for some time now. I just didn't know what, and I thought that letter might hold the answer. That's why I brought it to you. I had to find out.

EILÍS. When you handed me the letter, I felt my feet sink deep into the earth, and I couldn't move. I started thinkin' about all the things I'd have to leave behind.

BRIDGET. They're only things, Eilís.

EILÍS. No! They're much more than that. It's the table Da made for me with the wood from the cottage where we were born. The bed that the girls sleep in. The same one we shared growin' up. And this place—I think of all the winters when I poked the fire keepin' the flames alive. This is where Daniel and I began our lives together. It's the only place my children call home. It means somethin' to them and to me. I know every square inch of it like—like it's a part of me.

BRIDGET. *(Pause.)* What can you take?

(EILÍS pulls away from BRIDGET.)

EILÍS. Daniel says just the bare essentials—straw mattresses, cups, plates, cutlery, some clothes.

BRIDGET. *(Hiding her pain.)* I'll help you pack, and I'll make some of my little cakes to take on the ship. Your children are always beggin' me for 'em.

EILÍS. Bobby Fogarty told me that at the end of your voyage, you throw your mattresses overboard.

BRIDGET. No!

EILÍS. Must be a sight seein' hundreds of people throwin' their beds into the watery depths. Can you imagine how many are on the ocean floor? A final restin' place for the comfort of the fishes.

BRIDGET. It'll be quite an adventure.

EILÍS. Daniel wants us to see New York for a bit of time before we go to New Bedford. I'll see the places that he's written of all these years, like the Irish shantytown on Fifth Avenue.

BRIDGET. It amazes me that they give so many of their streets numbers instead of actually namin' 'em. I imagine in New York City you have to know how to count to find your way home.

EILÍS. They're buildin' this huge church, Daniel tells me— St. Patrick's Cathedral. Daniel says they've been buildin' it for twelve years, and it's only half finished.

BRIDGET. Soon, Eilís, you'll be writin' stories of America to me.

EILÍS. *(Looks out.)* I don't think in all of America they have the colors of Ireland. Lime washed walls changing colors with the light of day. The golden straw of the roofs. Fuchsia laden hedges blooming with "tears of God." Green hills rollin' down emptyin' into the silver sea—collidin' in a burst of foam. Does a person remember colors, do you think? Or do they fade along with the faces? Does Daniel remember any of this? Will I? *(Pause.)* Bridget?

BRIDGET. Yes?

EILÍS. I don't really have to go.

BRIDGET. What?

EILÍS. I could stay here.

BRIDGET. Eilís, you can't mean that.

EILÍS. I don't want to go to America. Who knows what I'll find when I get there. He writes stories about people and places I know nothin' of.

BRIDGET. *(Halfheartedly.)* Eilís, you've got to go.

EILÍS. I feel like I don't even know him anymore. All his letters are about America and his new life. I can't hear his voice in them anywhere. He just rambles about his search for work and the struggle he's made and the things he's learned.

BRIDGET. When he writes of his days, it's because he wants to share them with you.

EILÍS. And what about the crossin'? People die out there in the ocean, you know. I hear of it all the time. Ships breakin' up—collidin' with other ships.

BRIDGET. Eilís, people cross back and forth all the time.

EILÍS. You're the one that's filled Fionnuala's head with your stories of soul cages and shipwrecks! She'll be in a panic.

BRIDGET. I'll tell her that I made it all up.

EILÍS. And the sicknesses on board! No! I think my children would be safer here. *(Pause.)* Tell me I'm right, Bridget. Tell me I should stay.

(BRIDGET reaches out to EILÍS.)

BRIDGET. I wish I could, but I can't. Eilís, you have to go.

EILÍS. *(Pulls away.)* No!

BRIDGET. Are you really sayin' that you won't join him? After all the plans you made when he left?

EILÍS. I wasn't the one who decided he should go to America.

BRIDGET. It was a decision you made as husband and wife.

EILÍS. No! It was Daniel's.

BRIDGET. You're just scared.

EILÍS. Stop treatin' me like I'm a child! Don't you understand? I feel closer to the family next door than I do to my own husband. I cross the field to the O'Brien's or the McLellan's and our world is the same. I talk about my day, and they talk about theirs, and it's the same day. *(Pause.)* When Daniel writes of his days—none of them are mine. And, all this time he's spoken of New York, and now suddenly, he's travelled to Massachusetts. I feel like he's uprooted us all over again. Tell me the truth, Bridget, are you so sure that America will be better?

BRIDGET. I believe it will be.

EILÍS. With all those stories about the troubles people find when they get there? You've heard them! People livin' in flats ten to a room beggin' for food on the streets. That's not livin'.

BRIDGET. Eilís, you're not thinkin' this through.

EILÍS. Help me write him.

BRIDGET. Why? What will you say?

EILÍS. That I can't leave my family. I've got a home here!

BRIDGET. I can't help you do that.

EILÍS. I can't leave you! I won't let you become just a memory. I'm not goin' to America!

BRIDGET. You'll break his heart, Eilís. It's just selfishness. How will you live? The only way you've been survivin' is the money he's sent you from America. What would you do without that?

EILÍS. We'll think of somethin'.

BRIDGET. If that were true he would never have left in the first place.

EILÍS. We'll just work the land harder.

BRIDGET. You've worked it as best you could. It's full of rocks. There's nothin' more to come from it. Nothin's changed that. Everyone's strugglin' just to make enough to feed his family. Don't do this now that you're so close to havin' everythin' we ever dreamed of. *(Pause.)* Think, Eilís! He's been gone three years. What if he won't come home? Are you prepared to say good-bye to the man you love?

EILÍS. I don't even know how I feel about him anymore!

BRIDGET. You love him. I know you do!

EILÍS. How can you love someone halfway across the world? It's like lovin' a ghost.

BRIDGET. No! Lovin' Robert's like lovin' a ghost. Does Robert dyin' mean nothin' to you?

EILÍS. Robert's not dyin'. You said that just this mornin' he was a bit brighter.

BRIDGET. I made it up.

EILÍS. What are you sayin'?

BRIDGET. I told you a story from my head. You forget, I'm very good at stories, but there's no truth to it at all.

EILÍS. But why?

BRIDGET. I don't know why I said he'd reached out for me except that I wanted so much for it to be true. I want him to hold me like he used to. But he doesn't have the strength to share himself with me anymore.

EILÍS. Bridget, I'm so sorry.

BRIDGET. So when you say that Daniel writes to you describin' his life in America, I can't help but feel envious.

Robert's got nothin' left to tell me.

EILÍS. All the more reason I should stay—with Robert bein' so sick and your baby on the way.

BRIDGET. It's why you should leave. Give America a chance. Give our family a chance.

EILÍS. I wish he'd never gone to America.

BRIDGET. Don't say that. Robert could have gone with Daniel, but he didn't. He believed America was too big a gamble, so he chose the mines. I never said then what I felt. I wanted him to go with Daniel, but I didn't have the courage to tell him. But I'm telling you now. You've got to venture everythin' on America.

(Pause. EILÍS starts for the front door.)

EILÍS. It's too big a gamble. I've a letter to write.

BRIDGET. You're not even goin' to open his first?

(EILÍS turns back to BRIDGET.)

EILÍS. I don't have to read it. He told me he'd give me the passage information when next he wrote.

BRIDGET. I never thought of you as bein' a coward, but that's exactly what you are.

EILÍS. I'm not a coward. Can't you see that? I'm fightin' to stay.

BRIDGET. If you do, you'll lose everythin'.

EILÍS. I'm a grown woman with a mind of her own.

BRIDGET. You're makin' a mistake, Eilís. And I won't be a part of it. I've got to get home. *(She gathers up her things and begins to leave.)* I won't come back until you've read that letter.

EILÍS. Bridget! Bridget wait. All right! I'll open it. *(BRIDGET stops.)* But I'm tellin' you right now it won't change anythin'.

(BRIDGET moves back to the chair and sits. EILÍS opens the letter and begins reading to herself.)

BRIDGET. Out loud, if you please.
EILÍS. All right. *(Reads aloud.)*
My Dearest One,

How can I explain to you the joy this moment brings me. To finally say the sweet words that I've been workin' for, prayin' for, livin' for. I've set my mind and heart to but one task in these three years, one month and eighteen days—to bring my loved ones home to me.

I've been afraid I have, my dearest wife, to let you know that every day spent without you is filled with a sorrow so deep that I'd feared I might not make it to another day. That, perhaps, I should give up this dream of America and swim back to the warmth of your arms. Many a night I've stood at the port lookin' out to sea and callin' to mind the day when I will stand there awaitin' your ship to dock. I picture what your hair will look like. What you will be wearin'. What it will feel like to hold you in my arms again. The only thing that has kept me goin' is your dear picture. It's been the thread that stretches across the sea from my heart to yours. I want to be a husband to you again. I want to love you all the days of my life. I promise you just like I did that day in St. John's Church when we stood there lookin' for the future in each others eyes and sayin' the words that united us from that day forward—I promise to love, honor and cherish you.

I long to be a father to my children again—to Kathleen, Patrick, Brian and at last to Fionnuala. She's the special gift I've never seen that you'll soon be bringin' to me from Ireland.

You're to leave on the Algeria on the Cunard Lines on August the 12th.

BRIDGET. Oh, Eilís!

EILÍS. *(Continues reading.)*

You will go through immigration at Castle Garden where I will be waitin' for you, my love. From there we will go home as a family to New Bedford.

The front door of our home sets on the shore of the Atlantic Ocean. I am longin' for the day when we will walk barefooted in the sand, and I can show you the America I've found.

Till then, I hold your picture next to my heart till you are there to take its place.

BRIDGET. It's a lovely letter he's written you, Eilís.

EILÍS. Yes.

BRIDGET. The 12th of August. That doesn't give us much time does it?

EILÍS. No.

BRIDGET. But I'm sure that together we can manage it.

EILÍS. Bridget?

BRIDGET. Yes?

EILÍS. I've a powerful feelin' that if I leave, I will never see you again in this life.

BRIDGET. Oh, Eilís, don't you know that I'll always be with you? Wherever you are, I'll be the brightest moon that lights up your sky—when you look up at it and concentrate real hard, you might even hear me callin' your name.

EILÍS I won't need the moon to hear your voice.

BRIDGET. You and I, Eilís, will always hear the call of blood.

(They embrace.)

BRIDGET. In a way, the liberty you'll find in America is my liberty too. Knowin' that you will all be free gives me so much hope for the future of our family.

EILÍS. Please, Bridget, be careful.

BRIDGET. There's such a wind out there, Eilís. I can't say where I'm driftin' to. *(Removes the locket from around her neck.)* Here. Take my locket, and we'll put a photograph of me in it. It'll be our thread from Massachusetts all the way back to Ireland.

EILÍS. Not your locket. Mother gave that to you. You love it too much to be givin' it away.

(BRIDGET places the locket around EILÍS' neck.)

BRIDGET. Don't you know that when you give things away, you keep them forever.

EILÍS. I love you, Bridget.

BRIDGET. And I love you. *(Pause.)* Now, Eilís, you've got to go over to the McClellan's and tell the children your wonderful news.

EILÍS. Oh, you're right.

BRIDGET. I'll just stay here in case Fionnuala wakes up.

(EILÍS wipes her eyes.)

EILÍS. I don't want the kids to know I've been cryin'. *(Slaps both her cheeks.)* How do I look?

BRIDGET. You look lovely, Eilís.

EILÍS. All right then. I'll be right back. *(Pause. EILÍS starts to exit and turns back.)* Bridget, you won't leave before I return, will you?

BRIDGET. No, I'll be right here waitin' for you. *(BRIDGET watches EILÍS exit. After a moment, she waves as she continues to watch her cross the field and disappear from view. She lowers her hand.)* Oh, my Eilís, I will surely miss you all the days of my life.

(Lights slowly fade.)

END OF ACT I

ACT II
New Bedford, Massachusetts
1889

(Setting: A fishing town on the coast of Massachusetts. A cold evening in April 1889. The set consists of just the top of the roof of a weathered grey wooden house covering the entire stage. In the middle of the roof is a circular widow's walk. There is a trap door leading up to the walk. KATHLEEN CONNELLY WRIGHT stands alone looking out to sea. She is transfixed. She wears a long black dress with a high collar and long buttoned sleeves. She touches the cross on the chain around her neck. After a moment she unclasps the chain and takes it off. She connects the clasp and drapes the cross on the corner of the ledge of the widow's walk. She closes her eyes for a moment. Then with resolve she leans over the ledge. FIONNUALA CONNELLY KENNEDY opens the trap door and joins Kathleen. Kathleen quickly straightens up. Fionnuala is Kathleen's younger sister. She, too, wears all black. She carries a shawl in her arms. A gold cross and locket hang around her neck.)

FIONNUALA. I was thinkin' I'd find you here.

KATHLEEN. Where else should I be?

FIONNUALA. Downstairs with the others. There's a table full of cherished recipes down there.

KATHLEEN. I saw it.

FIONNUALA. And wouldn't you know it? Loreena McGinty has entrenched herself, she has, right along side the buffet table. If you don't come down soon, they'll be slim pickins'.

KATHLEEN. *(Pause.)* It's so calm tonight.

FIONNUALA. 'Tis. And just look at that moon! Much brighter than usual. Almost hurts your eyes to look at it.

KATHLEEN. Did you want somethin', Fionnuala?

FIONNUALA. No. I just came up for a breath.

KATHLEEN. All right, Fionnuala, take your breath then.

(KATHLEEN stares her down, and FIONNUALA takes in an exaggerated deep breath.)

FIONNUALA. I'll tell you, between Da's pipe and his huggin' the life out of me, I just had to get a way for a spell.

KATHLEEN. Da's still cryin' then?

FIONNUALA. He is. But you know Da. He won't admit to it. First it's the stove smokin'. Then it's somethin' in his eye. Anythin' but tears of sadness.

KATHLEEN. He loved Charlie.

FIONNUALA. Everyone did. *(Pause.)* Oh, I almost forgot. I brought you a shawl.

(FIONNUALA places the shawl around KATHLEEN's shoulders and steps away. KATHLEEN watches FIONNUALA

trying to keep herself warm.)

KATHLEEN. Looks to me like you're the one who needs warmin'. *(She removes the shawl and wraps it around FIONNUALA.)* Here—you take it.
FIONNUALA. I think you're right.
KATHLEEN. I don't feel the cold.
FIONNUALA. Well, I've always gotten the chill easier than you. *(Pause.)* Do you remember that time we went skatin' at Whisker Lake? You in nothin' but your linens. And me, piled so high in woolens I could barely stand up, let alone skate. But you—you were like a shootin' star. You set your blades to the ice and disappeared.
KATHLEEN. I'd rather be alone, if you don't mind, Fionnuala.
FIONNUALA. Kathleen Margaret! We no longer share a room you can be kickin' me out of. I'll be standin' beside you, if you please. *(Pause.)* You should see Jean. She has seized the opportunity, and she's chasin' Kevin round the room. And him, runnin' for his dear life! It's quite the spectacle. But she doesn't care who's whisperin'. She's got her mind made up, she has. She's decided our brother's the one, and there's no stoppin' her. I like her. I'm hopin' she wears him down. *(Pause.)* Really, Kathleen, you should be there to greet your callers.
KATHLEEN. They're not my callers.
FIONNUALA. Whose would they be then?
KATHLEEN. Charlie's.
FIONNUALA. You are bein' quite stubborn you are.
KATHLEEN. Finn?
FIONNUALA. Yes.

KATHLEEN. *(Pause.)* Have you prepared yourself?

FIONNUALA. Don't talk of such things!

KATHLEEN. There's no denyin' the possibility of it. Not now.

FIONNUALA. There's simply no preparin' for it. I watch him go out to sea, and I pray that he returns.

KATHLEEN. I prayed too, Fionnuala.

FIONNUALA. The good Lord makes his choices as he sees fit. I'm not sayin' it's fair—because it's not. I'm only sayin' we've got no voice in it.

KATHLEEN. No voice at all.

FIONNUALA. Everyone in town has been touched by this tragedy. So many people have lost a brother or a father... *(Pause.)* Eileen Martin told me this mornin' she's movin' away.

KATHLEEN. Is she?

FIONNUALA. Seems she has an uncle in Maine whose wife recently passed away. Eileen is goin' to live with him and help him raise his children.

KATHLEEN. She's very good with children.

FIONNUALA. She should be, she's enough of her own. I don't know how she keeps track of them all. I'm not sure her uncle knows what he's gotten himself into.

KATHLEEN. And the other widows? What are they goin' to do?

FIONNUALA. I haven't actually talked to all of them.

KATHLEEN. What about Maureen?

FIONNUALA. Movin' in with her sister, I think.

KATHLEEN. She won't be stayin' on in her house?

FIONNUALA. They were already pretty steep in debt from what I've heard. She wouldn't be able to come up with the monthly.

KATHLEEN. Sounds like there's been a lot of gossipin'.

FIONNUALA. Just concern. *(Pause.)* Well, maybe just a little gossipin'.

KATHLEEN. I haven't talked to the others since—

FIONNUALA. They'll be a lot of changes around here.

KATHLEEN. I expect so.

FIONNUALA. Frank and I have a bit of savins' if you find you need a little to get by, or we could—

KATHLEEN. That's very generous of you, Fionnuala, but please tell Frank, and Da, I won't be needin' it.

FIONNUALA. Well, the offer stands if you change your mind.

KATHLEEN. I won't.

FIONNUALA. Maybe we'll talk about it later.

KATHLEEN. He shouldn't even have been on the boat that day! He was feelin' under the weather the night before. I tried to convince him to stay home and rest, but you know Charlie.

FIONNUALA. You never could have talked him out of somethin' he'd set his mind to.

KATHLEEN. I walked him down to the dock. I wanted to make sure he wrapped himself warm. I watched him twist the muffler around his neck and tuck the ends into his coat. For my benefit, I expect. Halfway out he probably tossed it aside.

FIONNUALA. I saw his boat that mornin'.

KATHLEEN. You did?

FIONNUALA. I was lookin' out at the rain clouds wonderin' if I should put up the wash when his boat passed by the house. I waved, but they were all so busy toolin' the nets— no one saw me. *(Pause.)* I wish he'd seen me.

KATHLEEN. When those clouds blackened, I felt a knot in the pit of my stomach. Charlie had been out in bad weather before, but this was different. All that day and night, I could feel him battlin' the storm. But when the skies finally cleared, I couldn't feel him any more. As the days passed, all I could do was keep watch.

FIONNUALA. Waitin's the hardest part. Half your time's spent longin' for some word of him, and the other half fearin' it.

KATHLEEN. For the whole week that followed I could look around and see some of the other wives pacin' on their rooftops too. But one by one they all gave up the walk.

FIONNUALA. Because they'd made their peace.

(KATHLEEN walks around the widows walk looking out at the rooftops of the other houses.)

KATHLEEN. First Emily stopped comin' out, then Mary, then Eileen, and then, finally, Maureen—but I just couldn't.

FIONNUALA. Wouldn't you mean.

KATHLEEN. Won't.

FIONNUALA. This place is just bringin' you more sorrow.

KATHLEEN. Don't you think I know that?

FIONNUALA. Then why return to it day after day?

KATHLEEN. It's a compellin' perch, Fionnuala.

FIONNUALA. I understand that. I must have done the walk hundreds of times, but you don't have to anymore.

KATHLEEN. I was comin' here to pray, but I can't.

FIONNUALA. I'll get Father Halpin to come up.

KATHLEEN. He can't help me.

FIONNUALA. I know that he's been a great comfort to the other widows.

KATHLEEN. Then he can keep comfortin' them.

FIONNUALA. He's just downstairs. Let me bring him up.

KATHLEEN. No! I don't want to see anyone!

FIONNUALA. All right. *(Pause.)* You must admit Father Halpin said a nice mass. Don't you think?

KATHLEEN. I suppose.

FIONNUALA. And that poem he read. Beautiful. Just beautiful. "He will not come..."

KATHLEEN. *(Angrily.)* I don't want to hear it.

FIONNUALA. "... And still I wait..."

KATHLEEN. I said no!

FIONNUALA. I'm sorry.

KATHLEEN. *(Pause.)* Is Charlie's family still down there?

FIONNUALA. I think they may have gone, but I'm not sure, Would you like to go down and see?

KATHLEEN. No.

FIONNUALA. His Mother told me that you're welcome to stay with them, if you like.

KATHLEEN. I don't think so.

FIONNUALA. I told her that.

KATHLEEN. Thank you.

FIONNUALA. Da was thinkin' you might want to come and stay with him. For a couple of weeks maybe.

KATHLEEN. Oh, Fionnuala—

FIONNUALA. Just until you get your bearins'.

KATHLEEN. You and I both know that a couple of weeks would turn into years.

FIONNUALA. Not necessarily. Besides, it would be nice for Da and Kevin to have you around the house.

KATHLEEN. You said yourself that Kevin and Jean McDonnell are bound to marry.

FIONNUALA. I did, but it may not be that soon.

KATHLEEN. But he will leave eventually, and then it would just be me and Da.

FIONNUALA. You'd be a great comfort to him.

KATHLEEN. I'm too old to be Da's little girl again.

FIONNUALA. Well, if you want to stay here, perhaps you could take in lodgers.

KATHLEEN. I tell you all I want is to be left alone, and you suggest I take strangers into my home.

FIONNUALA. I had another thought. You make such wonderful breads. If I helped you, maybe together we could make enough to take to market and sell.

KATHLEEN. You do not want to be haulin' bread to market.

FIONNUALA. Why not? People do it all the time. We could both profit from it. Think about it, Kathleen. I know I have a good head for business. Why, I bet together we—

KATHLEEN. I hear you speakin', but it's Da's words I hear comin' out of your mouth.

FIONNUALA. It was just a thought.

KATHLEEN. If I close my eyes I can almost picture him wavin' at me from the boat.

FIONNUALA. Kathleen, your watch is over.

KATHLEEN. It's not the lookin' for him I'm doin'.

FIONNUALA. Then what are you lookin' for up here?

KATHLEEN. I thought there'd be somethin' left to hold on to. But I'm not findin' it.

FIONNUALA. Da will be worryin' about us.

KATHLEEN. About me, you mean. I know full well Da sent you up here to fetch me.

(FIONNUALA places her hand over the cross hanging from a

chain around her neck.)

FIONNUALA. Nothin' of the kind!

KATHLEEN. I always know when you're lyin'.

FIONNUALA. You don't know any such thing!

KATHLEEN. Since the day you understood lyin' was a sin, you would drape your hand over your cross just as you began your fibbin'. I do believe you think if you cover his image, God won't hear you.

FIONNUALA. First of all, I do not consider myself to be a liar.

KATHLEEN. I know that—

FIONNUALA. And secondly, Kathleen Margaret, I think it's quite frightenin' how well you know me.

KATHLEEN. Lyin's just not in your nature.

FIONNUALA. As it's not in yours to give up.

KATHLEEN. I'll be joinin' you later. *(Pause.)* Go downstairs, Fionnuala.

FIONNUALA. Da's got the fear in 'im that you're gonna do somethin'—somethin' crazy.

KATHLEEN. Go downstairs and tell him I'm fine.

FIONNUALA. It's not just Da. I see you sinkin' deep into despair, and it frightens me.

KATHLEEN. I won't deny it, Fionnuala. I embrace the idea of not feelin' this pain anymore. Not feelin' anythin'.

FIONNUALA. It's natural you should feel this way. We all know how deeply you loved him, but—

KATHLEEN. God's taken my Charlie. Until I met him I believed I'd never fall in love. There wasn't one man before him that stirred me like he did from the first moment I laid eyes on him.

FIONNUALA. I know that.

KATHLEEN. No you don't! No one does! No one knows how my heart raced as I watched him climb our porch steps. I thought to myself I'd never seen anyone so handsome.

FIONNUALA. I never told you this, but I was a bit frightened of him at first.

KATHLEEN. Well, he was a new face to us.

FIONNUALA. Just off the boat from Ireland—lookin' for his uncle's house. Carryin' that great big satchel across his shoulders. He looked so strong and tanned from the sun. And his accent was so thick—we almost couldn't understand him.

KATHLEEN. You kept turnin' to me askin'—

KATHLEEN.   FIONNUALA.
"What words are these?"   "What words are these?"

KATHLEEN. All I could do was shrug my shoulders in bewilderment, but Charlie was so patient with us. He kept repeatin' that address over and over—must've been twenty times. But he never stopped smilin'.

FIONNUALA. It was such a hot day, and he kept eyein' that cider. He must've drunk three pitchers of it. You used every last apple in the house makin' it.

KATHLEEN. Then when he left I raced up to the widow's walk and watched him stroll down the strand. He kept turnin' back—wavin' to me—and I kept returnin' his waves. I hated the thought of losin' sight of him.

FIONNUALA. But it wasn't long before he found his way back to our house. Two days later he returned with that same satchel—full of apples. He loved you from the start.

KATHLEEN. I've finally lost sight of him.

FIONNUALA. Please let us help you.

KATHLEEN. There's nothin' any of you can do.

FIONNUALA. Charlie would have no patience with this pityin' you've mired yourself in.

KATHLEEN. I'm no longer askin' you. I'm tellin' you. Go downstairs with the others. Leave us be.

FIONNUALA. You shame me, Kathleen.

KATHLEEN. I shame you then.

FIONNUALA. We are no strangers to death. We've lost two brothers and our dear Mother. And you—you've felt death's sting most of all, losin' your only child. Losin' your beloved Matthew.

KATHLEEN. I don't want to talk about my baby, Fionnuala.

FIONNUALA. Even when Matthew died, you didn't lose your faith.

KATHLEEN. Stop it, Fionnuala!

FIONNUALA. Even then you didn't—

KATHLEEN. Not one more word about Matthew!

FIONNUALA. I'm sorry... I just... I want you to listen to me.

KATHLEEN. I'm tired, Fionnuala. I'm so tired.

FIONNUALA. We're all sorry that you've lost Charlie. But, God help me, I'm afraid you're—(*Pause.*) We will all miss him deeply. He was as much a brother to me as Kevin or Brian. I know that Charlie would be very disappointed in you, Kathleen.

KATHLEEN. Go away!

FIONNUALA. It's freezin' out. Please come down. I'll make you a cup of tea, and we'll talk by the fire.

KATHLEEN. I feel closer to Charlie right here.

FIONNUALA. Kathleen, if you give up you abandon me and everyone else who loves you. The livin' are downstairs waitin' for you.

KATHLEEN. This has nothin' to do with anyone but me.

FIONNUALA. What about my daughters? What about Maggie and Nora? They love you so much, Kathleen. We all need you to hold our family together like you always have.

KATHLEEN. Not me. Mother was the one. She kept us together.

FIONNUALA. And when she couldn't—you did.

KATHLEEN. I was never as strong as Mother.

FIONNUALA. You're wrong.

KATHLEEN. Finn, please...

FIONNUALA. How about on the ship comin' to America? Ma was so sick, and you were the one who took care of us. You said I was terrifyin' everyone with my talk of soul cages and shipwrecks. You told me you'd sneak me up on deck on nights when the moon was bright, and together we'd beg the man in the moon to bring us all safe to America.

KATHLEEN. *(Pause.)* Five weeks it took us. I was afraid we might not make it. The seas were so rough—

FIONNUALA. So many of our friends have made the same journey over the years. The O'Briens, Davises, McClellans— they're all around us. Many of them are downstairs right now.

KATHLEEN. It's like God lifted up our whole valley and set it down halfway across the world.

FIONNUALA. I wish I could remember Ireland and the trip to America.

KATHLEEN. I'll never forget. Poor Danny Morrissey. He lost everyone in the crossin'.

FIONNUALA. And now he's downstairs sittin' with his youngest on his lap singin' songs.

KATHLEEN. The day we landed we all sang.

(FIONNUALA seizes the moment.)

FIONNUALA. Tell me what it was like.

KATHLEEN. Oh, Fionnuala, it was so long ago.

FIONNUALA. But it's my story too.

KATHLEEN. You must of heard it a hundred times.

FIONNUALA. Oh, at least a hundred, but I haven't heard it for such along time. Tell me again like you used to when I couldn't sleep.

KATHLEEN. Oh, Fionnuala, I really don't—

FIONNUALA. Please—tell me what it was like—seein' America for the very first time.

KATHLEEN. You are so stubborn.

FIONNUALA. It's a family trait. I get it from my older sister.

(KATHLEEN begins to tell the story by rote.)

KATHLEEN. When we first caught sight of the harbor everyone crammed on deck, gapin' in amazement at the tall buildins'. For a while no one spoke—all you could hear was the water and the sea gulls and the sound of the ship's engine slowin'. Then... *(Pause. Begins again with feeling.)* almost in a whisper a young man began singin'. Then someone else joined in—and another— and another—until every last one of us was singin'. We docked at the East River pier, and from there a barge took us to Castle Garden.

FIONNUALA. Ma told me I kept tuggin' at your skirt beggin' you to show me the Castle.

KATHLEEN. You kept sayin', rather indignantly, "That don't look like no castle to me."

FIONNUALA. But it must have to you.

KATHLEEN. Aye. *(Pause.)* But then the castle gates nearly didn't open for me.

FIONNUALA. What do you mean?

(KATHLEEN pauses, surprised she's spoken of it.)

KATHLEEN. I almost didn't make it through immigration.

FIONNUALA. I never knew this.

KATHLEEN. A very special secret just between Mother and me.

FIONNUALA. Why?

KATHLEEN. She didn't want Da to know what she'd gambled.

FIONNUALA. What happened? And don't leave out a word.

KATHLEEN. It was like the final Day of Judgment when you had to prove your worth to enter the heavenly kingdom. There were so many lines, so many instructions to follow, but you could go no further if you did not pass the medical inspection. None of you had been marked which meant you'd passed and could move on, but I'd an infection in my eyes. We'd heard that would be enough for quarantine on Ward's Island. Mother knew that Ward's Island was the first stop in a trip back home.

FIONNUALA. Oh, Kathleen...

KATHLEEN. The medical examiner poked at my eyes with an instrument like a button hook. Oh, how my eyes pained to the touch. Then he grabbed that piece of chalk. He pressed it firmly against my coat, and I could feel my fate etch across my chest as if burned into my skin. First the letter C—then a

t. It meant trachoma. It meant Ward's Island.

FIONNUALA. How did you get through then?

KATHLEEN. Mother grabbed his hand and without so much as a quiver in her voice she said, "My little girl's been cryin' the whole night, Doctor. Rubbin' her eyes raw. I expect you've seen many cases like this." And she slipped her life's savin's into his hand.

FIONNUALA. And he took it?

KATHLEEN. Oh, yes, he took it. I was only ten, but I understood what had transpired, and I kept silent. He stood there takin' us all in. Then he told me to remove my coat, quickly turn it inside out and put it back on. I was cleared. We gathered up our baggage and hurried away. We were almost to the door when the examiner called out, "Mrs. Connelly!" Mother stopped and quickly gathered us tight. I could feel her trembling as he drew near. Suddenly, he held out his hand and said in such a loud, clear voice, "Mrs. Connelly, I do believe you dropped this," and he placed her purse in her hand. Tears welled in her eyes. I'd never seen her cry but for that day. She thanked him, and we walked out of the dark into the warm sunlight.

FIONNUALA. Amazin'. Oh, how I wish I could remember. And Da was waitin' there for us, right?

KATHLEEN. Oh, yes. He was terribly handsome—dressed in a beautifully tailored black suit and top hat—which he'd borrowed for the occasion. It had been three years since we'd seen him.

FIONNUALA. Ma must have been so happy.

KATHLEEN. They held on to each other for such a long time. *(Pause.)* Then together we crossed the drawbridge that connected the island to the mainland. America! I thought that

I was the luckiest girl that had ever lived. That moment is like a picture in my mind. We were all so full of dreams.

FIONNUALA. You are my livin', breathin' history, Kathleen. You are my Ireland.

KATHLEEN. Tellin' the story to you now feels like thumbin' through a picture book.

FIONNUALA. It's been a hard struggle, but we're still here.

KATHLEEN But so many of us are gone. And now Charlie's left me.

FIONNUALA. Charlie didn't leave you, Kathleen. He died. He just died.

KATHLEEN. And I died with him.

FIONNUALA. I won't believe that—after all you've gone through—what we've all gone through. It's never been easy for us. When the boats were destroyed by the storm, we all went down to the docks, and together we built new ones— when half our street went up in flames, we built new homes...

KATHLEEN. You can't rebuild a life!

FIONNUALA. Yes you can! But it's not the dead that need rebuildin'—it's the livin'.

KATHLEEN. Leave me alone.

FIONNUALA. You've got to make another journey, Kathleen. But you don't have to cross an ocean to get there. You just have to come downstairs with me.

KATHLEEN. You're askin' for somethin' that I can't give.

FIONNUALA. I'm not askin' you—I'm beggin' you!

KATHLEEN. Please, Fionnuala—

FIONNUALA. You can't leave me, Kathleen. Don't you know I'd spend the rest of my life grievin' for you? *(Pause.)* Remember how Ma mourned the killin' of her only sister? *(Touches the locket that is pinned to her dress.)* All she had left of her Bridget was a picture—the picture in this locket, and she missed her every day of her life.

KATHLEEN. It's no use. I buried my heart with Matthew, and now my soul has drowned with Charlie.

FIONNUALA. I want you to listen to Father Halpin's poem, Kathleen.

KATHLEEN. I told you no.

(KATHLEEN turns upstage. FIONNUALA follows.)

FIONNUALA. You need to hear it.
KATHLEEN. No!
FIONNUALA.[1]
"He will not come, and still I wait.
He whistles at another gate
Where angels harken
Ah I know..."

(KATHLEEN corrects FIONNUALA's misquote.)

KATHLEEN. "Listen... where angels listen. *(She continues on with the poem.)*
Ah I know
He will not come
yet if I go
How shall I know he did not pass
Barefooted in the flowery grass?

The moon leans on one silver horn
Above the silhouettes of morn,

[1] "To a Little Boy in the Morning" by Francis Ledwidge

And from their nest sills finches whistle
Or stoopin' pluck the downy thistle.
How is the morn so gay and fair
Without his whistlin' in its air?

The world is callin', I must go.
How shall I know he did not pass
Barefooted in the shinin' grass?"

FIONNUALA. I'd hoped you'd heard it, and you did.
KATHLEEN. It was Charlie's favorite.
FIONNUALA. Do you believe that I love you?
KATHLEEN. You know I do—
FIONNUALA. Then let that be enough for now.
KATHLEEN. I don't know—
FIONNUALA. Come back to us, Kathleen.
KATHLEEN. *(Shivering.)* Oh, Fionnuala, I'm not sure—
FIONNUALA. You are my shinin' star, and I've bathed in your light all my life. But now I want to be the anchor that holds you here with us.

KATHLEEN. I find you are a great surprise to me, Fionnuala Bridget.

(FIONNUALA removes the shawl and places it around KATHLEEN's shoulders.)

FIONNUALA. Please, stay with me. Let me keep surprisin' you.

(KATHLEEN touches FIONNUALA's face.)

KATHLEEN. I do believe you just might do that.
FIONNUALA. I'm sure of it.
KATHLEEN. I just don't know how to start over again.
FIONNUALA. You begin by tearin' yourself away from this place. It's no longer your walk, Kathleen. Leave it. Leave it for someone else.
KATHLEEN. Will you hold my hand?
FIONNUALA. For as long as you like.

(FIONNUALA takes KATHLEEN's hand. KATHLEEN takes the cross from the corner of the widow's walk and holds it tightly in her hand. They begin to exit. KATHLEEN stops and takes one last look up at the moon.)

KATHLEEN. The moon really is brighter tonight, isn't it?
FIONNUALA. That it is, Kathleen. That it is.

(They descend the stairs. Lights slowly fade.)

END OF ACT II

ACT III
New York City
1911

*(Setting: Union Meeting Hall, New York City, March 31, 1911.
A wooden table sits upstage left in an empty meeting hall.
A podium sits upstage center, and both a union and an
American flag are displayed upstage right. MAGGIE
KENNEDY enters from the back of the hall and walks down
through the audience. Maggie's a union organizer, and her
weary face reflects the hardships of union work. She wears
a hat and a thin coat. She crosses to the stage and places a
briefcase on the table. She walks downstage and stares out
at the house as she removes her coat. Though her dress is
worn, she has chosen her best dress for this important day.
She crosses back to the table and lays her coat down. She
then drags the podium downstage left. She exits the stage.
NORA KENNEDY FITZPATRICK enters from the back of
the hall through the audience. She calls out Maggie's name,
but gets no response. She continues up the aisles. Just as she
is about to climb the stairs to the stage, Maggie reenters
carrying a tray with a pitcher of water and several glasses.
Nora stops and retreats back into the shadows. Maggie sets*

51

down the tray and grabs her papers. She crosses to the podium and begins to rehearse her speech.)

MAGGIE. About a year ago many of you here counted your voices among the twenty thousand who struck for the union. We didn't know then how hungry, how cold—how lonely those thirteen weeks would be. *(Pause. She rubs her eyes, checks her notes and begins again.)* We lost the fight at the Triangle Shirtwaist Company. The workers there went back without union recognition. Because we lost in the Triangle, last week in a fiery twenty minutes, one hundred and forty six of our voices were silenced forever. I watched as Rosalie and Lucia Maltese went together. *(Stops. Removes her hat and stares at it, then goes back to the speech.)* So did Sara and Sarifine Saricino. Fifteen year old Jennie Franco—went alone. I saw one girl toss off her hat and throw coins into the air. *(Pause. To herself.)* Who was she? *(Crosses to the table and puts down her notes and hat and faces upstage.)* Who was she?

(NORA calls out from the darkness.)

NORA. Maggie?

(MAGGIE slowly turns around. For a moment she is too stunned to speak.)

MAGGIE. Nora? *(NORA moves closer.)* My God! Nora! *(MAGGIE runs to NORA, and they hug.)* What are you doing here?
NORA. Mama's very sick, Maggie.

MAGGIE. What? What's wrong?

NORA. She's had another heart attack.

MAGGIE. What do you mean "another"—?

NORA. She had one last May, but she recovered from it.

MAGGIE. No one told—

NORA. She was never quite as strong, but we thought—

MAGGIE. No one told me.

NORA. She didn't want you to know.

MAGGIE. Why?

NORA. I'm not sure. She made us all promise to keep it from you.

MAGGIE. In all her letters, she never let on.

NORA. Two days ago she had another.

MAGGIE. My God—And you've come all this way to—Why didn't you send me a telegram?

NORA. I needed to see you—to tell you in person.

MAGGIE. It's so hard to take in. *(Notices the locket around NORA's neck and touches it.)* You're wearing Mama's locket.

NORA. Mama gave it to me on my wedding day.

MAGGIE. I used to love to make her open it and tell me the story of Grandmother's voyage to America. It felt like every time she told it, she lived it all over again. Mama loved that story.

NORA. The locket should have been yours.

MAGGIE. *(Pause.)* It doesn't matter.

NORA. It means a lot to me.

MAGGIE. I just can't believe you've come all this way by yourself.

NORA. I'd never even rode a train before today.

MAGGIE. Where's your husband?

NORA. Back home.

MAGGIE. It's good to see you again, Nora.

NORA. You look so tired, Maggie.

MAGGIE. I haven't gotten much rest since the fire.

NORA. What fire?

MAGGIE. Last week in the Triangle Shirtwaist Company. So many women lost their lives—so many of my friends.

NORA. We don't have much time, Maggie.

MAGGIE. Yes... I'll get away as soon as I can.

NORA. What?

MAGGIE. I'm sure that in a few days, I can—

NORA. Haven't you been listening? You need to come now.

MAGGIE. Nora, I can't.

NORA. I'm not going home without you, Maggie! I told everyone I'd bring you back with me.

MAGGIE. You don't understand the situation, Nora.

NORA. Maggie! She could be dying.

MAGGIE. I'm sorry, Nora, but I just can't.

NORA. I'm risking not being there myself to make sure that you are.

MAGGIE. I told you, I'll come home. I just need some time.

NORA. If you don't come now, you may never see her again. There's no time left.

MAGGIE. It's just that right now it's very difficult to get away.

NORA. Maggie, you've been saying that for two years.

MAGGIE. I have responsibilities here, Nora.

NORA. You can't come home when it's convenient for you. Not this time. (*Pause. Calmly.*) We are your family, Maggie. And our Mother is very sick. You've got to be there at her bedside. Nothing could be more important than Mama.

MAGGIE. I know that, but I've—
NORA. *(Angrily.)* Get your things together, Maggie! Our train leaves in an hour.
MAGGIE. All right, Nora.

(MAGGIE slowly moves over to the table and picks up her coat.)

NORA. I think you should know that I went to your apartment first.
MAGGIE. You did?
NORA. Yes.
MAGGIE. I see.
NORA. He told me where to find you.
MAGGIE. So—you met Sam.
NORA. I met him.
MAGGIE. He's a good man, Nora.
NORA. I'm sure he is. *(Pause.)* Does he live there?
MAGGIE. No. He lives in Chicago. He's President of the United Garment Workers Union. He travels a lot—but he stays with me when he's in New York.
NORA. I was stunned when a man opened your door. *(Pause.)* Are you in love with him?
MAGGIE. I care for him very much.
NORA. What does that mean?
MAGGIE. No. I'm not in love with him.
NORA. *(With great difficulty.)* Does he sleep in your bed?
MAGGIE. *(Pause.)* Yes.

(They each simultaneously make the sign of the cross.)

NORA. How can you do that?

MAGGIE. Because there are times when I need someone to hold me.

NORA. I thought you were beyond caring about things like that.

MAGGIE. No. I'm not beyond that.

NORA. Then why don't you marry him?

MAGGIE. I don't love him for one reason.

NORA. Why not find someone you do love and get married?

MAGGIE. Because it's just not possible.

NORA. Of course it is.

MAGGIE. Not for me.

NORA. Haven't you ever been in love, Maggie?

MAGGIE. I was very much in love once. But he wanted marriage and children. I can't do my job and be somebody's wife and mother.

NORA. What happened to him?

MAGGIE. *(Pause. Softly.)* He asked someone else. She said yes.

NORA. You used to dream about getting married.

MAGGIE. Now I have other dreams.

NORA. I don't see why marriage can't still be one of them. Don't you want someone to take care of you?

MAGGIE. What do you think, Nora? I should marry someone, and he'll take care of me for the rest of my life?

NORA. I'm talking about security.

MAGGIE. Security? Tell that to the women who work fourteen hours a day right along side their husbands—and their children.

NORA. Get your things together, Maggie.

MAGGIE. Please, Nora, I just need a little time.

NORA. I told you. There is none.

MAGGIE. There are two hundred women coming to hear me speak today.

NORA. Won't there be other union people here?

MAGGIE. Yes, but—

NORA. One of them can give a speech.

MAGGIE. It's not that easy, Nora. There are a lot of things I want said. I want my voice to be heard. It's so important for the future of the union.

NORA. Your speech is written down, isn't it?

MAGGIE. Yes, but—

NORA. Then leave it for them to read.

MAGGIE. These women depend on me. I've never let them down before.

NORA. Well, now they'll really feel like family.

MAGGIE. Nora—

NORA. Well, it's true. But you are not going to let us down now! You can't be that heartless.

MAGGIE. Nora, I'm afraid that if we don't spur them into action now, everything we've worked so hard for will be lost. I'm just asking for a little time to finish setting up the room and organize my notes. No one will be able to understand my speech if I don't talk to them first.

NORA. *(Pause.)* When are they coming?

MAGGIE. In a few minutes.

NORA. *(Pause.)* All right, we'll wait fifteen minutes, then we're leaving.

MAGGIE. *(Starts marking up her notes.)* You're not the little girl I remember.

NORA. You've changed too. *(Pause.)* You cut off all your beautiful hair.

MAGGIE. Yes. *(Touches her hair.)* It's not very fashionable.

NORA. From what I've seen today, anything goes in this city. There was a woman sitting on the stoop of the building next door to yours wearing the strangest hat. It had long purple and yellow feathers that hung down from the brim and covered her eyes!

MAGGIE. On the block she's known as the "pro..." *(Thinks better of what she is about to say and edits herself.)* ... "the hat lady."

NORA. Do you know her?

MAGGIE. Just to wave hello. People come and go so much in the neighborhood, you don't get a chance to really know many of them. They seem to wind up getting distinguished by their appearance or their manner—like "the hat lady" or "the man who whistles." God, that's how I know the majority of them.

NORA. Sounds like quite a neighborhood.

MAGGIE. You know, Grandfather Daniel lived on that very same block when he came from Ireland—just a few doors down from me.

NORA. Really?

MAGGIE. You must have passed right by his building on your way here.

NORA. How do you know where he lived?

MAGGIE. Aunt Kathleen told me. Do you remember him much?

NORA. I remember how his eyes would brim with tears whenever he spoke of Ireland.

MAGGIE. Of course he always blamed the tears on the smoke from his pipe.

NORA. Oh, his pipe! He'd fill it with tobacco and let me light it. I thought it was magic.

MAGGIE. Maybe it was a bit of magic that drew me to that same street. We both came to New York searching for something. Sometimes I sit on the stoop of his building, and I look out on the street and wonder what he must have thought about.

NORA. About the family he left behind, I suppose.

MAGGIE. Or the future.

NORA. Do you give many speeches?

MAGGIE. Not a lot—not compared to Rose Schneiderman. She started giving speeches at sixteen. Can you imagine that? She can set up an apple box on any street corner, and within minutes, people are applauding. By the end, there isn't a lapel in the crowd not bearing a union button.

NORA. Rose Schneiderman. I remember that name. She's the one who made you run away.

MAGGIE. I didn't run away, Nora. I ran toward something.

NORA. Will she be here?

MAGGIE. No. She's speaking at another rally at the 22nd Street Hall. This has been a week for grieving, but now it's time to strike back.

NORA. So you knew a lot of those girls?

MAGGIE. Almost all of them. Oh, Nora, I have been to so many funerals this week. I went to one that had a carriage load full of flowers and hundreds of mourners and a brass band leading the hearse. This morning I went to Julia Rosen's. She didn't have any of that. She was buried while her three children and a few neighbors wept. Most of them are like Julia's.

NORA. I'm sorry, Maggie

MAGGIE. You should have seen the funeral procession yesterday. Over one hundred thousand women marched. All I could hear for hours was the rain and the sound of feet slogging through the streets. The headline read, "The Skies Wept." And they did.

NORA. Heaven help them.

MAGGIE. You make me think of that Marie Dressler song, "Heaven will protect the working girl."

NORA. God protects us all, Maggie.

MAGGIE. Is that so? Then where was God on March 25th? Where was God when the doors were locked behind those women? Management was afraid they'd sneak out for a smoke or steal some of their needles. They were trapped in the building, Nora. I can't get it out of my mind. I saw my sisters jump from the windows.

NORA. Your "sisters?"

MAGGIE. My union sisters. We picketed together through a bitter winter trying to get a union shop in there. That strike was the worst I'd ever seen. The company hired sluggers to "intimidate" us.

NORA. Why didn't you call the police?

MAGGIE. Let me assure you, Nora, the police are not on the side of the union. In the end the Triangle workers went back without union recognition. The company never even heard our demand for open, unlocked doors.

NORA. Surely, someone... the government will listen to your demands now.

MAGGIE. Why should they? We're women! We can't even vote. How can you have a political system that runs a country where one half of its strongest voices are never heard?

NORA. This sounds very much like speech making,

Maggie. Am I talking to my sister or the union organizer?

MAGGIE. They're one and the same.

NORA. I don't want you to talk about these things when you come home.

MAGGIE. Why?

NORA. It will just upset Mama.

MAGGIE. That's not true! She believes in what I'm doing here. She always has.

NORA. You'd better get your notes together, Maggie. Your "sisters" will be here soon.

MAGGIE. Yes. *(She goes back to her notes.)* Will you tell me about everyone?

NORA. What do you want to know?

MAGGIE. How's Aunt Kathleen?

NORA. She's fine.

MAGGIE. And her bakery?

NORA. There's always a line around the block.

MAGGIE. Really!

NORA. Did you know Bridget just started working behind the counter?

MAGGIE. No! Bridget? When I left she was still playing with dolls.

NORA. Well, our little sister's all grown up. But she has a devil of a time figuring out the change.

MAGGIE. That may explain the long lines!

NORA. You may be right.

MAGGIE. And the boys? How are they?

NORA. Brendan and Jack are still working hard in the mill. Brendan's little boy is just about a year old now. Ryan's got a new boat. It's all he talks about. He swears he's going to have his own fishing fleet before he's thirty. You know, he just might.

MAGGIE. And you?

NORA. Me? Well, I'm still getting used to being married. It's been hard since Mama got sick. I find myself torn between my household and hers.

MAGGIE. I'm sure you're doing your best.

NORA. *(Pause.)* Maggie, do you ever miss me?

MAGGIE. Of course I do.

NORA. But you never came back.

MAGGIE. I couldn't, Nora. I'm fighting this war all the time.

NORA. There is no war, Maggie.

MAGGIE. Oh, yes there is—even if you can't hear it in New Bedford.

NORA. This life had made you hard.

MAGGIE. I learned quickly that if you don't put your feelings aside, it'll break your heart.

NORA. What did she say?

MAGGIE. Who?

NORA. Rose Schneiderman. What could she have possibly said to make you give up everything?

MAGGIE. When Rose came to New Bedford to speak, every word she said touched something in me. As if I'd been waiting all my life to hear those words. She helped me find my voice. Rose gave me a chance to do something—to make a difference.

NORA. You could've done this work in New Bedford.

MAGGIE. Nora, the world is much bigger than that. Can't you see that I live for the union? That I dream for the union?

NORA. Yes, I can. But I don't understand it.

MAGGIE. When I first got here, I went to a striker's home and met her children. The company had asked her to come back to work, but she refused to desert the union. I asked her how she could bear such hardship, and she said, "If I cannot give my children bread, I can give them liberty." That's what I am fighting for.

NORA. But why do they have to come first all the time?

MAGGIE. How can I make you understand what's happening here? It's too late to help those women who died in the Triangle, but it's not too late for the rest of my sisters and their children. Nora, women are working fourteen hours a day earning $4.00 a week. Clocks are set back so they won't know how long they've worked. Paychecks are "shorted" because they're charged for electricity, the boxes they sit on, coat lockers, needles—anything—anything to keep the worker suppressed.

NORA. *(Angrily.)* Do I have to walk a picket line to get you to care about me?

MAGGIE. Of course not!

NORA. *(Suddenly.)* I—I don't feel well.

(MAGGIE gets NORA a chair.)

MAGGIE. Here, sit down. I'll get you some water.

(MAGGIE picks up the pitcher and pours a glass of water.)

NORA. It was a long train ride.

(MAGGIE gives NORA a glass of water.)

MAGGIE. Yes, yes. Now drink this.

NORA. Thank you. It's very stuffy in here.

(MAGGIE helps NORA off with her coat.)

MAGGIE. Let's get your coat off.

NORA. *(Suddenly blurts out.)* I'm going to have a baby.

MAGGIE. What? My little sister is going to have a baby? Nora, that's wonderful! How far along are you?

NORA. Well, I've been sick every morning for about two months.

(MAGGIE runs for her purse.)

MAGGIE. I think I have a piece of bread in my purse.

NORA. Maggie, I'm pregnant—not hungry.

MAGGIE. Oh,—yes. *(Looks at NORA and smiles.)* You look beautiful, Nora. Really beautiful.

NORA. Thank you. *(Pause.)* Maggie, I want to tell you something, but I'm afraid you'll just think I'm crazy.

MAGGIE. What?

NORA. I thought I saw you yesterday in New Bedford.

MAGGIE. What are you talking about?

NORA. I was in Aunt Kathleen's shop looking through the glass at the loaves of bread, and suddenly, I wasn't looking through the glass anymore. I was seeing my reflection in it. But it was your face that I saw. I turned around expecting you to be there, but you weren't. I just burst into tears. Everyone in the shop was staring at me. Then Aunt Kathleen announced to the crowd, "She's with child." They all nodded their heads as if that explained my behavior. But I swear I saw you as clear as I do right now.

MAGGIE. Maybe you did.

NORA. That's when I knew I had to see you.

MAGGIE. I'm glad you came, Nora. Are you feeling better now?

NORA. Yes, I'm fine.

MAGGIE. Mama must have been so happy to hear your news.

NORA. She was.

MAGGIE. I can't believe you took so long to tell me about the baby. You never were one to keep a secret.

NORA. That's not true.

MAGGIE. Oh, really?

NORA. I keep a very good secret!

MAGGIE. Is that so?

NORA. It most certainly is.

MAGGIE. How about the time we skated past the ropes at Whisker Lake?

NORA. What?

MAGGIE. You were out ahead of me, showing off, and the ice started to crack?

NORA. Oh, yes! And you were yelling at me to come back, but I was too scared to move. I was sure that if I took even the smallest step, the ice would give way.

MAGGIE. I knew you wouldn't come on your own.

NORA. I think I'd already said twenty Hail Mary's by the time you reached me. You took my hand and ordered me not to let go no matter what happened. I was so amazed that you actually whistled the whole way back. How could you have been so calm?

MAGGIE. Calm? I was scared to death. I only whistled so you wouldn't hear the ice cracking. Then when we got back to the boathouse, we made a solemn vow not to tell Mama or Dad. I don't think we were in the house three seconds before you blurted out the whole story.

NORA. I couldn't help myself. The moment I saw Mama I burst into tears.

MAGGIE. And I wasn't allowed to skate again that whole winter.

NORA. If you recall, I took your punishment right along side you. I didn't skate the rest of the winter either.

MAGGIE. It wasn't because you were afraid to get back on the ice?

NORA. Well, that too. *(Pause.)* You saved my life that day, Maggie.

(Pause. MAGGIE picks up newspaper clippings about the fire.)

MAGGIE. But I didn't save theirs. No, I didn't save theirs.

(Long pause.)

NORA. We can't wait any longer. We've got to catch that train. *(She crosses and picks up MAGGIE's coat and holds it out to her.)* Here, take your coat.

MAGGIE. I'm sorry, Nora. I can't go back with you.

NORA. Maggie, you've got to.

MAGGIE. I believe if I stay here and stir these women today—we can save so many lives.

NORA No! You said you'd come!

MAGGIE. And as soon as I can, I will.

NORA. Mama needs you at home now!

MAGGIE. She doesn't want me to give up this fight. It's why she never wanted me to know she was sick in the first place.

NORA. No!

MAGGIE. She knows I can't do anything for her.
NORA. We all need you to come home!
MAGGIE. You've come because you need me.
NORA. Yes, but—
MAGGIE. You'll have to continue to take care of the family on your own, Nora.
NORA. No, I won't let you do this!
MAGGIE. You've never really forgiven me for leaving, have you?
NORA. Of course I have.
MAGGIE. It's time for the truth. Why are you here?
NORA. I told you. Because of Mama.
MAGGIE. I don't think that's altogether true. There's more, isn't there?
NORA. No. There's nothing more.

(MAGGIE grabs hold of NORA.)

MAGGIE. We're back on Whisker Lake, and the ice is cracking all around us.

(NORA struggles to free herself.)

NORA. I don't know what you're talking about.
MAGGIE. You want me to save you again, don't you, Nora?
NORA. Of course not!
MAGGIE. Say it!

(NORA tries to pull away from MAGGIE, but MAGGIE will not let her go.)

NORA. Let go, Maggie.
MAGGIE. I won't let you go until you say it.
NORA. No. Stop it!
MAGGIE. If you don't tell me now, we'll both drown in it.
NORA. Stop it!
MAGGIE. Say it, Nora!! Finally say it!

(NORA breaks away.)

NORA. I hated you! I hated you for leaving me! You left me a letter. A God damn letter! Then, I thought if I made it to the station before you left, I could make you stay. I ran as fast as I could, but I didn't make it. *(Begins to cry.)* I watched from the top of Quincy Hill as your train moved away.

(MAGGIE moves toward NORA.)

MAGGIE. Nora, I had to leave.

(NORA moves away.)

NORA. Then when you wrote that you would come to my wedding, I thought maybe it was time to forgive you. You said you were coming home for me. You sounded like the old Maggie again. And when your arrival time came and went, I still made everyone wait. And then I just couldn't wait anymore. You were supposed to stand beside me that day.
MAGGIE. I'm so sorry.
NORA. Why is everything more important than me? What were you doing that you couldn't at least have sent word you weren't coming?

MAGGIE. I had every intention—

NORA. The world is full of good intentions, Maggie.

MAGGIE. *(Pause.)* I was in prison, Nora. Two days before your wedding, I was arrested on the picket line and sent to Blackwell's Island. One of the scabs had a stick and started hitting one of the girls, and I had to help her.

NORA. Oh, Maggie—

MAGGIE. They took us to the police station. One of the officers said he saw lice in my hair. Then he grabbed some scissors and started hacking. That's the first time I realized that my screams were useless. We were sentenced to ten days. They classified us as prostitutes, and so we were put in cells with other prostitutes. They tried to break my spirit, and they almost succeeded. But I kept thinking of you. You in Mama's white dress and lace veil, and I was there. I was standing right beside you, and I was holding your hand. I thought if I closed my eyes and pictured it hard enough, I'd be there. And I was. You helped me escape.

NORA. Why didn't you tell me?

MAGGIE. I wrote Mama about it.

NORA. Mama knew you were in prison?

MAGGIE. I tell her everything.

NORA. I can't believe it. Does she know about Sam?

MAGGIE. Well, almost everything. *(Pause.)* The day I told Mama I was moving to New York—she cried, but she said she saw something in me. A kind of fever. She's never stopped loving me, but she's let me go. I don't think you have yet.

NORA. I thought we'd always be together.

MAGGIE. In our hearts we're always together. You're taking such good care of the family, and they're going to need you more than ever. You've got to go back home, Nora, and you've got to leave me here to take care of my other sisters.

(NORA picks up her coat and purse.)

NORA. I miss you so much, Maggie.
MAGGIE. And I miss you every day.
NORA. You don't know how much I've wanted to hear you say that.

(NORA and MAGGIE embrace.)

MAGGIE. You tell Mama I love her.
NORA. I will.

(NORA takes a few steps, lightly slaps both her cheeks and takes a deep breath. She stops for a moment and undoes the clasp to her locket. She turns and crosses back to MAGGIE. She starts to put the locket around MAGGIE's neck.)

MAGGIE. No, Nora— *(NORA manages to get it around MAGGIE's neck.)* But you...
NORA. When you give things away, you keep them forever. *(MAGGIE kisses NORA's hand. NORA breaks away.)* Come home when you can, Maggie.

(NORA exits.)

MAGGIE. *(To herself.)* Good-bye, Nora. *(MAGGIE fights back her tears and softly begins rehearsing her speech. Pauses, then gathers up her strength and continues.)* We lost the fight at the Triangle Shirtwaist Company. The workers there went back without union recognition. Because we lost in the Triangle, last week in a fiery twenty minutes, one hundred and forty six of our voices were silenced forever. And those of us who are left behind must keep holding onto each other. We've got to work harder than ever. We can never let it happen again. They were burned or suffocated or jumped to their death that afternoon. They had never had a fire drill. There were no sprinklers. The fire escapes bent and twisted and broke from the weight. The factories here are not... *(She pauses and touches the locket. She steps away from the podium and moves closer to the audience. She begins again—from the heart.)* I'll never forget what I saw that day. I was only blocks away when people started running past me, toward Washington Park. And suddenly, I found myself running with them. Running blindly. Then I heard the screams. I looked up, and through the smoke I thought someone was throwing bales of dresses out the window. When it landed I saw that it was two young girls. I looked up again and saw girls lining the ledges on the ninth floor. Some of them were already burning. But for them, there was no other escape. And so they leapt. Bodies were falling all around me. When the fire engines got there, I watched them crank the ladder, but it stopped at the sixth floor. We were all screaming, "Raise the ladders! Raise the ladders!" But they couldn't go any higher. And so they kept jumping. The firemen's hoses flooded the streets, and the gutters ran red with their blood. I saw sisters leap arm in arm—holding on to each other until the last. Rosalie and Lucia Maltese. Sara and Sarifine Saricino. Fifteen year old Jennie Franco went alone. And there was this one girl. She threw off her wide brimmed hat, and watched it float down. She opened her purse and tossed coins high into the air. Then she lifted her arms—

as if to fly away. As if she no longer needed her earthly possessions. This beautiful angel took flight and found freedom. I couldn't hear the screams anymore. I couldn't hear anything. When I looked up again, all I saw were angels. I watched them drop their earthly bodies, and their spirits soared above the flames. And all my sisters must soar above the flames. We must carry on and never, never give up the fight because this is the legacy we leave our sisters and daughters and all their daughters to come, and for us that fire still burns.

(Lights slowly fade.)

END OF PLAY

PROPERTY LIST

ACT I

Rustic outdoor table
Clothesline
Clothes pins (12)
Tattered clothes (to hang on clothesline)
Old chairs (2)
Crate (slatted, large enough for 2 to sit)
Old sewing basket
Pin cushion
Needles
Patches of material
Dress patched with several different pieces of material
Wooden spools of thread
Serving tray (big enough to hold next 5 items)
Tea pot or old beat up copper kettle
Metal mugs (2)
Tin of milk
Tin of sugar
Spoons (2)
Old tin for money
Assorted pieces of appropriate paper and coin money
Baskets (2) (to carry groceries)
Groceries (potatoes, item wrapped in butcher paper)
Bunch of wilted beets
Posted, cancelled, sealed envelope (New Bedford to
    Ireland)
Hand-written letter (will be read out loud)

ACT III

American flag (hanging)
Shirtwaist Union flag (hanging)
Table
Several wooden chairs (to be set up)
Podium
Coat Rack
Union signs (at least 1)
Easel
6" stack of half sheet flyers
Tray (large enough for next 2 items)
Small pitcher
Water glasses (3)
Briefcase (old, leather, beat-up)
Writing pad
Pencils
Brown folders (5)
Newspaper clippings (cut out articles about the fire) (15)
Hand-written copy of final speech

COSTUMES

<u>ACT I (as appropriate for 1869)</u>

EILÍS   Long apron w/pockets
                     Blouse
                     Long skirt

BRIDGET   Shawl
                     Long skirt
                     Pregnancy pad
                     Worn brown boots
                     Locket on ribbon

<u>ACT II (as appropriate for 1889)</u>

FIONNUALA Long black dress
                     Shawl
                     Cross on chain
                     Black button boots
                     Locket pinned to dress

KATHLEEN   Long black dress
                     Cross on chain
                     Black button boots
                     Handkerchief

<u>ACT III (as appropriate for 1911)</u>

MAGGIE   Tattered light coat
              Wide brimmed hat
              Hat pin
              Handbag
              Shirtwaist
              Long skirt
              Low heels
              Watch on long chain

NORA   Overcoat
              Long dress
              Low heels
              Hat
              Gloves
              Purse
              Tapestry carpet bag
              Locket on chain

Racing Demon
DAVID HARE

"Riveting."
NEW YORK MAGAZINE
"David Hare ... can shake a soul."
TIME MAGAZINE

This award-winning play premiered at the Royal National Theatre and at Lincoln Center. Attracting unwanted publicity, the Church of England is racked with dissention over matters of doctrine and practice and is at odds with the government. Reverend Lionel Espy and his team of clery struggle within this volatile climate to make sense of their mission in South London. Winner of four prestigious "Best Play" awards. 8 m., 3 f. (#19956)

Sacrilege
DIANE SHAFFER

"A play charged with genuine ideas."
WCBS TELEVISION
"Compelling. SACRILEGE moved me to tears."
VARIETY

Ellen Burstyn starred on Broadway in this riveting drama about a devout Catholic nun who is fighting the Vatican to allow women in the priesthood. Her evenutal expulsion from her order forces others to re-examine the meaning of faith, spiritual violence and the redeeming grace of God. 6 m., 3 f. (#20977)

Samuel French, Inc.
SERVING THE THEATRICAL COMMUNITY SINCE 1830

OTHER PUBLICATIONS FOR YOUR INTEREST

COASTAL DISTURBANCES
(Little Theatre- Comedy)

by TINA HOWE

3 male, 4 female

This new Broadway hit from the author of *PAINTING CHURCHES, MUSEUM,* and *THE ART OF DINING* is quite daring and experimental, in that it is *not* cynical or alienated about love and romance. This is an ensemble play about four generations of vacationers on a Massachusetts beach which focuses on a budding romance between a hunk of a lifeguard and a kooky young photographer. Structured as a series of vignettes taking place over the course of the summer, the play looks at love from all sides now. "A modern play about love that is, for once, actually about love--as opposed to sexual, social or marital politics . . . it generously illuminates the intimate landscape between men and women." --NY Times. "Enchanting."--New Yorker. #5755

APPROACHING ZANZIBAR
(Advanced Groups—Comedy)

by TINA HOWE

2 male, 4 female, 3 children --Various Ints. and Exts.

This new play by the author of *Painting Churches, Coastal Disturbances, Museum,* and *The Art of Dining* is about the cross-country journey of the Blossom family--Wallace and Charlotte and their two kids Turner and Pony--out west to visit Charlotte's aunt Olivia Childs in Taos, New Mexico. Aunt Olivia, a renowned environmental artist who creates enormous "sculptures" of hundreds of kites, is dying of cancer, and Charlotte wants to see her one last time. The family camps out along the way, having various adventures and meeting other relatives and strangers, until, eventually, they arrive in Taos, where Olivia is fading in and out of reality--or is she? Little Pony Blossom persuades the old lady to stand up and jump up and down on the bed, and we are left with final entrancing image of Aunt Olivia and Pony bouncing on the bed like a trampoline. Has a miracle occurred? "What pervades the shadow is Miss Howe's originality and purity of her dramatic imagination."--The New Yorker. #3140

THE FILM SOCIETY
Jon Robin Baitz
(Little Theatre) Dramatic comedy
4m., 2f. Various ints. (may be unit set)

Imagine the best of Simon Gray crossed with the best of Athol Fugard. The New York critics lavished praise upon this wonderful play, calling Mr. Baitz a major new voice in our theatre. *The Film Society*, set in South Africa, is *not* about the effects of apartheid—at least. overtly. Blenheim is a provincial private school modeled on the second-rate British education machine. It is 1970, a time of complacency for everyone but Terry. a former teacher at Blenheim, who has lost his job because of his connections with Blacks (he invited a Black priest to speak at commencement). Terry tries to involve Jonathan, another teacher at the school and the central character in this play; but Jonathan cares only about his film society, which he wants to keep going at all costs—even if it means programming only safe, non-objectionable, films. When Jonathan's mother, a local rich lady, promises to donate a substantial amount of money to Blenheim if Jonathan is made Headmaster, he must finally choose which side he is on: Terry's or The Establishment's. "Using the school as a microcosm for South Africa, Baitz explores the psychological workings of repression in a society that has to kill its conscience in order to persist in a course of action it knows enough to abhor but cannot afford to relinquish."—New Yorker. "What distinguishes Mr. Baitz' writing, aside from its manifest literacy, is its ability to embrace the ambiguities of political and moral dilemmas that might easily be reduced to blacks and whites."—N.Y. Times. "A beautiful, accomplished play . . . things I thought I was a churl still to value or expect—things like character, plot and theatre dialogue— really do matter."—N.Y. Daily News.   (#8123)

THE SUBSTANCE OF FIRE
Jon Robin Baitz
(Little Theatre.) Drama
3m., 2f. 2 Ints.

Isaac Geldhart, the scion of a family-owned publisher in New York which specializes in scholarly books, suddenly finds himself under siege. His firm is under imminent threat of a corporate takeover, engineered by his own son, Aaron, who watches the bottom line and sees the firm's profitability steadily declining. Aaron wants to publish a trashy novel which will certainly bring in the bucks; whereas Isaac wants to go on publishing worthy scholarly efforts such as his latest project, a multi-volume history of Nazi medical experiments during the Holocaust. Aaron has the bucks to effectively wrench control of the company from his father—or, rather, he has the yen (Japanese businessmen are backing him). What he needs are the votes of the other minority shareholders: his brother Martin and sister Sarah. Like Aaron, they have lived their lives under the thumb of Isaac's imperiousness; and, reluctantly, they agree to side with Aaron against the old man. In the second act, we are back in the library of Isaac's townhouse, a few years later. Isaac has been forcibly retired and has gotten so irascible and eccentric that he may possibly be *non compos mentis*. His children think so, which is why they have asked a psychiatric social worker from the court to interview Isaac to judge his competence. Isaac, who has survived the Holocaust and the death of his wife to build an important publishing company from scratch, must now face his greatest challenge—to persuade Marge Hackett that he is sane. "A deeply compassionate play."—N.Y. Times. "A remarkably intelligent drama. Baitz assimilates and refracts this intellectual history without stinting either on heart or his own original vision."—N.Y. Newsday.   (#21379)

Other Publications for Your Interest

PRECIOUS SONS
(LITTLE THEATRE—COMIC DRAMA)
By GEORGE FURTH

3 men, 2 women—Interior

This finely wrought new play is a real rarity these days: an original play, originally produced on Broadway. Ed Harris and Judith Ivey starred in this autobiographical drama about a family struggling to make it economically in the late 1940's in Chicago. The father, Fred Small, has a chance for a promotion, which would necessitate the family move to another city. The youngest precious son, Freddy (really the central character), is caught between his desire to be a professional actor and his father's determination that he finish high school and go on to college. Set against everyone is the mother, Bea, who has her own ideas about how the family should be run. "This seemingly innocuous play turns out to contain an emotional force that approaches terror. It's the terror that comes when we realize we don't really know 'the truth'. Is Bea the monster she seems . . . Is Fred an insensitive hulk who deserves to have his dreams trampled by a wife he's unwittingly repressed? Where does love fit into all this—who really loves whom, and how do they love?"—Newsweek. "Furth creates convincing people: he gives them clever, well-wrought and wholly plausible dialogue; and he appreciates the timeless give-and-take of family life, its perilous candor and its resilience."—Time. "Furth has written wonderfully real characters. And given us a play about real things. Honest emotions. Couched in comedy."—WABC-TV. "Powerfully personal . . . A powerful family play . . . has an authentic, gripping dramatic logic that makes its climax seem surprising but inevitable."—Newsweek. (#18159)

SO LONG ON LONELY STREET
(LITTLE THEATRE—COMIC DRAMA)
By SANDRA DEER

3 men, 3 women—Interior

Audiences and critics alike cheered this excellent new play by a talented new American playwright both in its premiere production by Atlanta's Alliance Theatre and in its pre-Broadway tryout. It also had a short but respectable Broadway run. Set in a rundown old southern house situated on 25 acres of valuable land, the play is about the gathering of the Vaughnum family for the reading of crochety old Aunt Pearl's will. The secrets of three generations of the family are revealed slowly as the current generation tries to decide who is the rightful owner of the property. "A richly-textured work about a disputed inheritance, miscegenation, unrequited incestuous love and greed masquerading as Christian righteousness. Sounds heavy and sensational, but *Lonely Street* is neither. It's a funny and poignant human comedy . . . Southern gothic with a sense of humor and lots of heart."—Variety. "This play would tear the house down *anywhere*. It's just plain wonderful."—Atlanta Journal. "A winner."—Boston Globe. "Zesty, poignant and fiercely funny."—Time Mag. (#21254)